Reach for the Stars

If it is to be,
It is up to me!

Inspirational Poems for Anyone Who Is Blossoming

Written and Illustrated by

Leslee Ann Michaels

Happy Heart Press

Lake Fairlee, Vermont

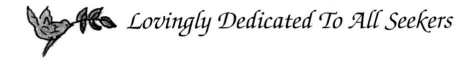 *Lovingly Dedicated To All Seekers*

Fourth Printing 2002

Text and illustrations copyright © 1997 Leslee Ann Michaels

Cover Design by Lightbourne Images
Cover Illustration by Leslee Ann Michaels

Published by Happy Heart Press
A Division of Happy Heart Cards Inc.
Lake Fairlee, Vermont 05045
800/603-9024   802/333-4667 (Fax)

Library of Congress Cataloging-in-Publication Data

Michaels, Leslee Ann
Reaching for the Stars: If It Is To Be, It Is Up To Me!
Inspirational Illustrated Poems for Anyone Who is Blossoming
p.   cm.
ISBN 1-890059-66-8

1) Inspiration—Poetry. 2) Self-esteem. 3) Personal Growth, English.   I. Title.
PS3525.5343 1997   811'.54   96–080052

Printed in Hong Kong

First Edition

10 9 8 7 6 5 4

Bookstore Distribution:
Login Publishers Consortium (LPC Group)

Gift Store Distribution:
Sourcebooks

PRELUDE

As diamonds are buried deep within the earth
and
pearls are hidden within the oyster beneath the sea
so
each of us has a treasure within

waiting to be discovered.

ACKNOWLEDGMENTS

Working on this book was a labor of love that gave purpose and meaning to my life. To all those very special people whose encouragement made it possible for me to write this book, more thanks than I could ever express.

To Michael, my best friend and forever love, I couldn't have done it without you.

To my Mom, Dad, and sister Lori, for all your love and support.

To my beloved Grandma Lee, who always believed I'd write a book one day. One day finally came.

To Linda, for tirelessly typing and retyping ever new drafts, you brought it all together.

To Laura, my mentor, for being the first to recognize I was a diamond (in the rough).

To Beth Wilkins, Andree Blumstein, and Ann Flood, for their loving insights which helped shape the book.

To Ginny Muff, for constantly reminding me "with God all things are possible!"

And to my students everywhere, thank you for all your appreciation.

Remember; those who reach, touch the stars!

CONTENTS

Aim High

Walking Small, Walking Tall

The Search

Born to Win

Making a Difference

Joy and Pain

Lessons

Letting Go

Blessings

All I Want for You

Aim High

CHOICES

Only we can choose
if we will win or lose.
We steer our own course,
let's do it without remorse.
Our life is about choices that we make,
and the chances we do or do not take.

I choose to live true to my inner vision.

I BELIEVE

I believe
I can change
my whole life
by the thoughts
I choose to think.
It really is up to me
to be whatever I want to be.

SELF-LOVE, RESPECT AND ESTEEM

With self-love, respect, and esteem
you'll feel worthy of any dream
though impossible it may seem.

Remember
Dr. Martin Luther King?
He inspired a nation
with his dream.

He is a great example
for us all to see,
for he fulfilled his destiny.

Teaching others
that education
is liberation
from discrimination.

It is good
to find a hero,
one you can admire.
Let their accomplishments
fill your hungry soul with desire,
then go ahead
and aspire,
you could be
as good as
he or she!

HEROINES AND HEROES

There are heroines and heroes all around
in every corner of the world they can be found.
This is the thing that they teach
goals and dreams are within reach.

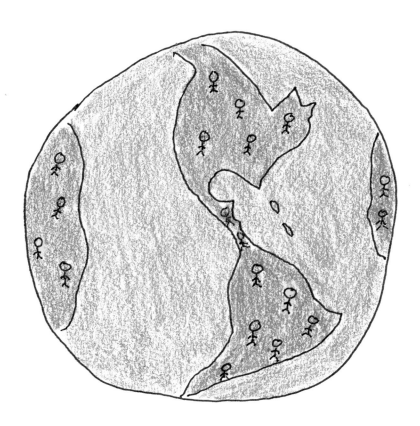

 *Within me is the same potential for achievement
as in my greatest heroes!*

AIM HIGH

Aim high
you'll be soaring
your life won't be boring.
Too many people's potential is never achieved
because they doubt and refuse to believe.

Don't worry about failure
you can reach the sky.
Worry about the chances you miss
when you don't even try.

Walking Small, Walking Tall

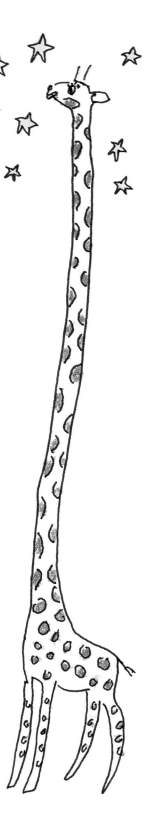

OLD WOMAN

She sat alone
in the dark
and wondered why
the life
she lived
had been a lie.

For too quickly
it flew by.

Then she broke down
and cried
wondering why
she never tried
and sadly alone
with her tears
she died.

It was too bad
and really quite sad
the poor old woman never had
the courage to try
to spread her Heartwings . . .

and FLY!

When I get to the end of my life,
I will have no regrets!

DRIFTER

My life was
drifting by.
Then one day
I wondered why
I wasn't flying high,
and I began
to cry.

I know what I want and where I am going.
My life has direction!

DEAD

I don't want
just a job
to survive
where I am
STUCK
at work
from nine to five
'cause that makes
me feel more DEAD
than alive!

It's a cryin' shame
that I played that game
and I've got no one to blame!

BUT,
one thing's for sure
I WON'T play it
ANYMORE!

I do work that I love,
so I'm loving what I do.

BLOSSOM, TWINKLE AND SHINE

Suppose the Rose
should hang her head
and say, "I don't want to blossom
in my flower bed."

Think of all we would miss,
the Beauty and the Bliss
of a Rose in Full Bloom.

Suppose a Star
up in the sky
said, "Why bother twinkling
when I'm up so high."

Think of all we would miss,
the Magic and Splendidness
of a Shining Star.

Suppose a Child
Tiny and Small
said, "Why bother dreaming
when I'm nothing at all."

Think of all we would miss,
if he or she didn't follow their bliss.
The world wouldn't be as bright
for there'd be one less spark of light!

WALK TALL

If you hold your head down low
it's hard to know the way to go.
Hold your head up high
enjoy a piece of the pie.

It's there for the taking
as is your dream for the making.
Life can be a feast
for the hungry beast.

Why think small
when you could walk tall
and life can be a ball
for one and all!

I replace doubt and fear,
with FAITH and CONFIDENCE!

The Search

SEARCH

Who am I?
What do I
want to do
to be true
my whole life through?

My task is to discover who I am,
then as fully as possible, to BE who I am!

YOU CAN BE

You can be
whatever you want to be
just do what comes naturally
you're as free as the wind.

First you've got to start
by listening to the song in your heart
and make it a special part
of every day.

Then when your soul sings
that's the time to spread your wings
just let go of your fright,
and you'll be in flight!

Like the birds and the bees
and the butterflies . . .
You'll Fly High
on the Wings of your Dreams.

*I feel a sense of joy,
mastering my own life!*

MAGIC

You've gotta click
with what makes you tick.
Find that secret spot
inside of you that's hot.
Then don't ever let it go,
for like Magic it will flow.
If you let it blossom and grow
such bliss and happiness
You Will Know!

*I discover my passion,
so my life is love in action!*

LISTEN

I've learned
to listen
to my own
inner voice
so I could
live the life
of my choice.

17

TRUST

Listen with your heart
all the answers
are inside of you.
Then TRUST what you hear
is really true.

*My power lies within me.
I can trust myself.*

STAR

You are a star
burning bright.
Within you
is the light,
of the world.

My time to shine is NOW!

BELIEVE

You have to believe in yourself
with a belief that is so strong
nothing can make it go wrong.
There are people who will try
to knock you down
you've got to pick yourself up
and turn yourself around.
There are people who will try
to steer you off course.
Be true to yourself,
not to any outside force.

Born to Win

BORN TO WIN

Don't be afraid to fail
if you try and never give up you will prevail.
You're a winner
born to win
roll up your sleeves and just begin.
The world will be a better place because of you
and all the wonderful things that you will do.

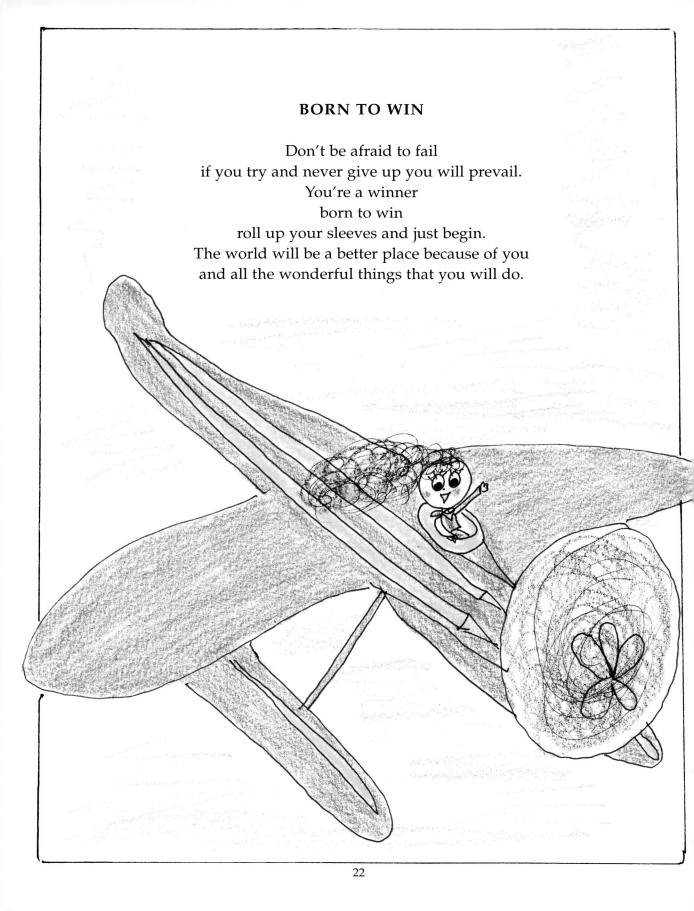

DO IT

I don't think it's good
that any woman should
DEPEND ON A MAN
WHEN SHE CAN
DO IT ON HER OWN!!

Believing I can, makes me half way there!

23

TRYING

It's easier said
than done
to stick with your dreams
and not run.

Especially when
the going gets tough
and the waters are rough
and you think
you've had enough,

But keep on
TRYING!!

*I hold on to my dream until it's no longer a dream,
but a beautiful reality!*

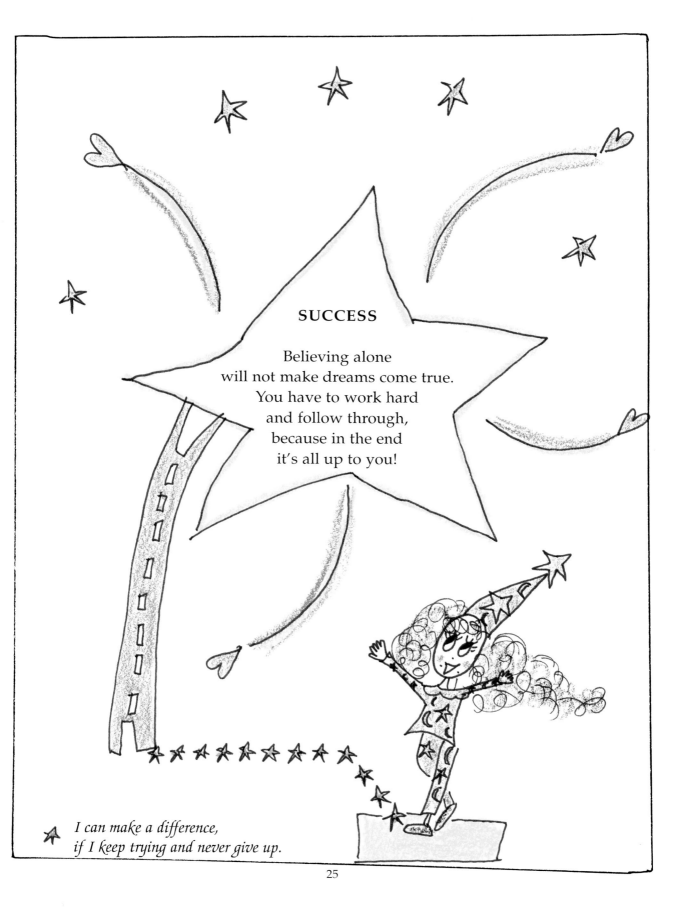

SUCCESS

Believing alone
will not make dreams come true.
You have to work hard
and follow through,
because in the end
it's all up to you!

*I can make a difference,
if I keep trying and never give up.*

25

GIVING MORE

I want more
than to just
earn a living
with my life
I want to be
GIVING,
GIVING MORE
MUCH MUCH MORE!

The more I have, the more I have to give.
The more I give, the richer my life is to live.

SYMPHONY

There is a song
inside of me
it sounds just like
a symphony.

It lifts my spirit
each time I hear it.

I love listening
to the song

inside of me!

I hear the song inside my heart,
and I sing it to the world!

SECRET

I've got a secret
I want to tell.
If you do
what you love,
you'll do it well!

*Everyday is lovely,
when I am doing what I love!*

Making a Difference

MAKING A DIFFERENCE

Living in vain
isn't the name of the game.
Doing for others
your sisters and brothers
helping people out
that's what it's all about.
There are so many things you can do
by giving, you'll be growing too.

MY OFFERING

If I could stop one heart from hurting
do something to lessen the pain,
my life will be worthwhile
I'll have not lived in vain.

If I can turn around despair
by showing someone that I care,
helping them to cope
by offering a little hope,
my life will be worthwhile
if I can turn one tear
into a smile.

LIVING LOVE

If you want to live love
you have got to give love.
Living Love
is Giving Love
Every Day!

Joy and Pain

VICTIM

Victim,
tossed into a stormy sea
of pain and misery,

You're a victim!

Your life's gone wrong
is the name of your song
been that way all along,

You're a victim!

Nothin's right
It's struggle and fight
You can't see the light,

You're a victim!

Blame! Blame! Blame!
Is the name of your game
Poor Poor Me,
guess that's how it has to be,

You're a victim!

You survive
but you're barely alive,

You're a victim!

I wish
you could see
beyond your own misery,
then you would know
there is another way to go.
It's your choice
do you choose to be,

A victim?

 *I replace self-contempt with self-love,
and watch my world turn around!*

This piece was based on a true experience I had with a teenage girl living on the streets of LA.

Introduction

(She was sitting there
with her long and dirty blond hair
on the curb in the street
with no shoes on her feet.)

15

"You don't have to stare, WITCH!"

I do stare
because I care.
I wonder what made you
so down and blue.

Drunk
like a skunk
in the middle of the day.
What in the world made you that way?

It does seem like you're only 15.
So very young
your life has just begun.
Why aren't you having fun?

I'm sorry,
    I stared.

Forgive me,
    I cared.

If I could've given that homeless girl anything, I would've given her this . . .

RAINBOW

I saw a triple
rainbow set
as I stood outside
on the grass that was wet,
with my bare feet.

Rainbows Remind Me
To Never Accept Defeat!

You should've seen
the bright colored arches
against the blackened sky.
It was so beautiful,
it made me cry!

Behind every cloud the sun is shining.

JOY AND PAIN

My life is like chocolate;
Bittersweet.
I've known the glory
of winning,
and I've suffered defeat.
Always within my joy,
some sorrow's been known.
Always within my smile,
some sadness is shown.
You can't have a rainbow
without sunshine and rain.
You can't live life
without joy and pain.

I WANT TO LIVE

I want to live
as if each day were my last
in the present,
not in the past.
I want to laugh
until I'm red in the face.
I want my life filled
with truth, beauty and grace.
I want to love
with all my heart
and make each day
a brand new start.

Lessons

RISE 'N SHINE

After I took
a good long look
into my eyes,
I began to realize
my problems weren't
curses and lies
but angels in disguise
giving me an opportunity . . .

to Rise n' Shine!

LESSON

Look for the lesson
that's to be learned
each and every time
that you get burned
and then you will see
why this is your reality.

I learn and grow from all my experiences!

FORGIVENESS

Forgiveness is a blessing,
a gift of heavenly grace.
It frees me of my past
so the pain I can erase.

I got rid of self-pity.
I got rid of blame.
Criticism and misery are no longer my name.

I've changed my tune.
I'm singing a new song.
Now I'm looking for the right,
instead of the wrong.

I'm choosing the best,
and releasing the rest!
Love is the key,
that set my heart free!

Letting Go

TODAY

I don't believe
I need to continue to grieve
for yesterday
when it's really true
the past is through.
So why carry it with you?

What's the point in carrying on
when the day is over and gone.
My yesterday I just let go
so today I could come to know.

After so many years
with bitterness and tears
I finally know
the only way to grow

IS TO JUST LET GO!

Why should I
shed another tear
for the day
that is no longer here?

'Cause tears get in the way
of my seeing for today.

I look around me
and I can see
a lot of people
living in misery.

It's really sad
how many people go through
their lives mad
thinking of the good
they could have had.

And whatever for
when nothing matters more,

than TODAY!

OVER

Is it right
you two should fight
all day and night?

Your love is over.
Let It Go!
So freedom and joy
you both can know.

Say good-bye
if you want to
cry but why
go on and fight
all day and night.
It doesn't seem right.

Your love is over.
Let It Go!
So new love
you both can know.

REMEMBRANCE

Your passing away
will sadden me everyday.
I will miss,
your love and kindness
and all the loving things
you used to say
and how you loved me
in every way.

I must accept with grace
that I will no longer see
your beautiful, smiling face.

From earth you are now gone
yet cherished memories of you
will live on forever in my heart.

And in my grieving
it helps me believing
your spirit is now free
for all eternity.

So, whenever I start crying
(and I often do
when I think I've lost you),
I wipe away the tears
from my eyes
because I know
true love, never dies!

Blessings

BLESSED

I feel blessed,
when I think
of the many things
that make my
heart sing.
I feel blessed,
when I sit down and cry
without asking why
until my eyes run dry.
I feel blessed,
when I laugh
until I cry
it's the all time high
to roar and soar
until I feel pain no more,
I feel blessed.

And when my world
looks like a mess
I sit down and think of
all the good I can bless.

Then it doesn't look so bad
after I've counted the blessings
I have had,
I feel
Blessed.

MENTOR

Countless hours
you spent
my teacher, healer,
and friend.

With limitless love,
understanding and truth
you opened so many doors.

Old soul
brightest light
example
of what we all
could be . . .

You mean so very much
to me.

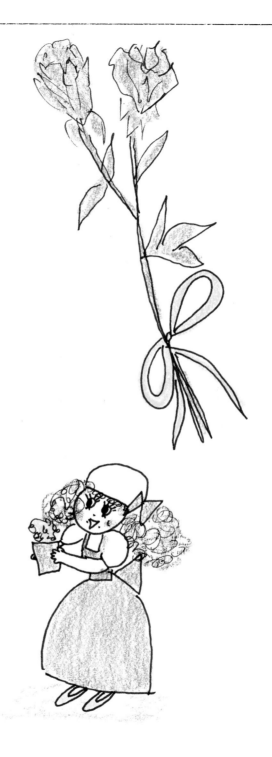

 I choose role models who bring out the best in me.

FRIEND

You're so beautiful
inside and out.
You make me smile
whenever I pout.

You care about how I feel
a friend like you is for real.

Rare and true
I'm happy to have
a friend like you.

For ours is a friendship
that will never end.
You'll always be
My Forever Friend.

DIFFERENT

I love to find
things that are one of a kind.
It stimulates my mind
and excites me,
because I'm different.

Ask anyone who knows me
and you will see,
they'll all agree
unanimously.

I'm as different
as different can be!

Most people are like sheep
but I'm no 'Little Bo Peep.'
I don't care
what designers say to wear.
I wear what I like
because I'm different.

When people go one way
I usually go the other,
I don't like to follow
my sister or brother.

I don't care what people say
I am happy to go my own way.

Because I'm different,
and happy to be so!

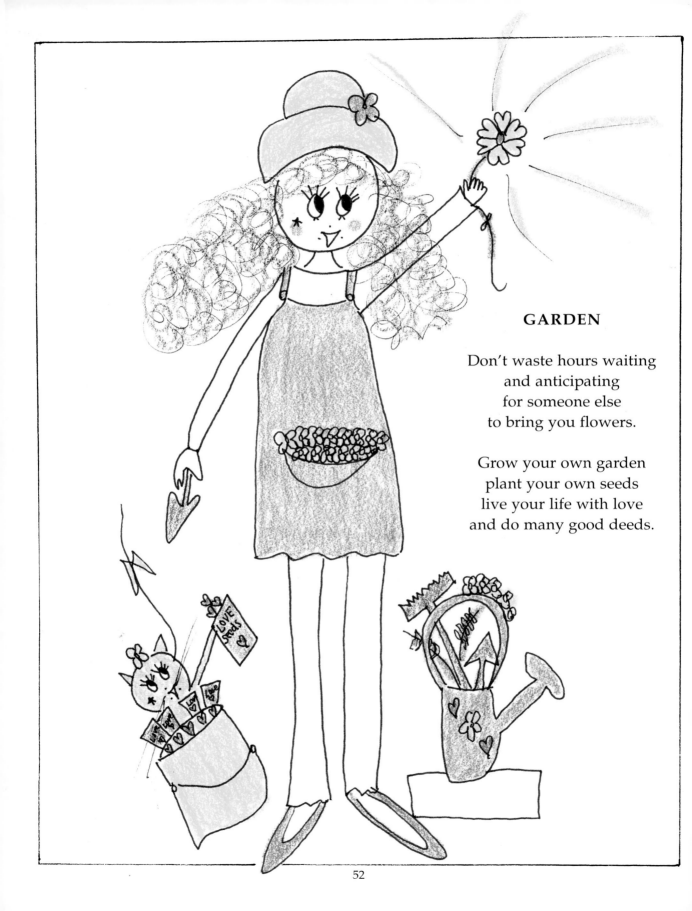

GARDEN

Don't waste hours waiting
and anticipating
for someone else
to bring you flowers.

Grow your own garden
plant your own seeds
live your life with love
and do many good deeds.

All I Want for You

THE BEST

All I want is for you to be
the very best
you can be.
Can't you see
how much that means to me?

TREASURE

No more
am I stuck
in a bottle
on the ocean floor.

This lost treasure
has been found
because the right
people were around
to help me
set myself free.

Could you imagine
how rich this world
would be,
if not a single soul
were lost at sea?

So many treasures around
waiting to be discovered
and found.

Have you found the
Treasure Within You?

If I seek I'll find my treasure,
and have many gifts to give to the world!

DREAM WEAVER

Life is too precious
to let moments pass.
Like sand in an hour glass
it goes by so fast.

By believing in miracles
and dreams that come true,
I've turned sand
into STARDUST
and so can you!

*There is no limit to
what I can accomplish!*

NO DRESS REHEARSAL

This moment is your life.
Fill it with pleasure,
let go of strife.

The curtain's up
and don't you know
it's YOU who is the STAR of the show!
Like a star, you're shining bright.
Filled with Love, filled with Light!

Now that you've put all fears aside
get on that thing they call life;
and RIDE, RIDE, RIDE!

BLOSSOM

Every seed
does need
a time to grow
before it will show . . .
A BEAUTIFUL BLOSSOM.

 May we all blossom through love!